All Mixed Up

The events in a story take place in a certain order, or sequence. Clue words such as *first*, *next*, *then*, and *finally* help the reader to determine the sequence.

Number these sentences in their correct order.

_____ Soon the day of their trip arrived.

_____ To warm up before the race, he slowly jogged one mile.

_____ First, April and Lisa wanted to go to Yellowstone National Park on vacation.

_____ Then he joined the other runners at the starting line.

_____ Then they looked at the brochure and made reservations.

_____ On the day of the race, he got up at 6:00 A.M.

_____ Finally, they drove to Yellowstone National Park.

_____ First, Mark signed up to run the 10K Old Town race.

_____ Next, they called the park to have a brochure sent to them.

_____ Finally, a horn blared and the race began.

_____ They packed their clothes and put them in the car.

_____ After the jog, he stretched his muscles.

_____ They received a travel brochure in the mail.

_____ Next, to train for the race, he ran every day for three months.

© Frank Schaffer Publications, Inc.   1   FS-11011 Fifth Grade Activities

Most Important

The **main idea** of a passage is the sentence that states the most important thing about the topic.

Read each passage. Choose the sentence that states the main idea of each passage.

---

1. Thomas Edison was one of the greatest inventors. His inventions changed the lives of many people. He tried to invent things that would not easily break down. He invented over 1,000 devices. He invented the electric light and the phonograph.

    ○ Thomas Edison invented over 1,000 devices.

    ○ Thomas Edison was one of the greatest inventors.

    ○ Thomas Edison invented the electric light.

---

2. Saturn is the sixth planet in our solar system and is the second largest planet. Saturn has many thin, flat rings around it. The rings are made up of snow, ice, and cosmic dust. It takes Saturn about $29\frac{1}{2}$ earth years to orbit the sun. There are many interesting facts about Saturn.

    ○ There are many interesting facts about Saturn.

    ○ Saturn is the sixth planet in our solar system.

    ○ Saturn has many thin, flat rings around it.

Animals Near the Water

Supporting details are the facts and information that explain or give examples of the main idea.

Read each main idea and the sentences that follow it. Write an **X** before each sentence that gives supporting details.

1. All species of shrimp have the same general body structure.

    ___ The largest part of a shrimp's body is its fan-shaped tail.

    ___ Shrimp have five pairs of legs.

    ___ Some people eat shrimp.

    ___ Shrimp have long, narrow bodies.

2. The sea horse is very different from most fish.

    ___ The sea horse's shape is very unusual—a stocky body with a long, coiled tail.

    ___ The sea horse swims in an upright position rather than a horizontal position.

    ___ It is covered with a kind of shell rather than scales.

    ___ Sea horses can be found in shallow waters along the coasts.

3. One of the most interesting features on a starfish is its arms.

    ___ The starfish may be red, violet, or greenish yellow.

    ___ The arms help the starfish to see.

    ___ The starfish can regrow an arm if it gets broken off.

    ___ Under each arm, there is a double row of small, movable tubes.

A Case for Detective Sardelli

When you are reading, you may come across words you do not know. A way to figure out the meaning of these words is to look for context clues. Look at the words in the sentence and in surrounding sentences to find clues to the meaning of the new word.

Choose a word from the magnifying lenses that can take the place of the boldfaced word in the sentence. Write the letter in the blank.

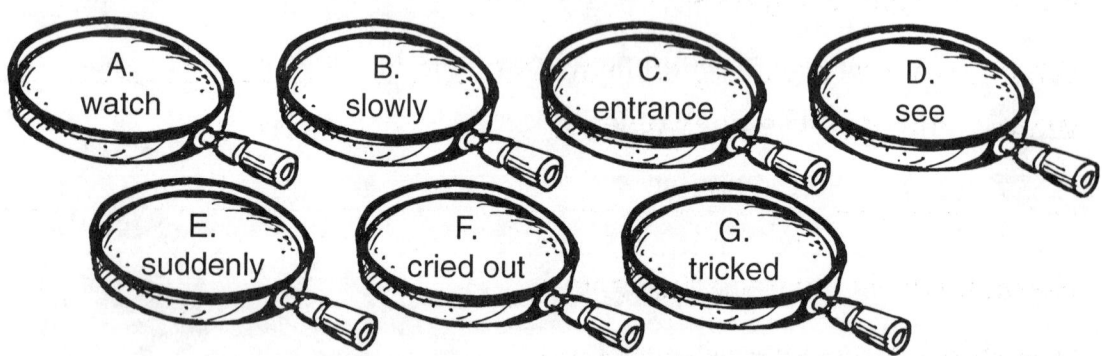

A. watch
B. slowly
C. entrance
D. see
E. suddenly
F. cried out
G. tricked

1. Detective Sardelli will **surveil** _____ Bert, the suspect, in order to uncover evidence.

2. Detective Sardelli hid in a dark alley where Bert could not **detect** _____ him.

3. Bert **abruptly** _____ turned and moved toward the alley.

4. At the **ingress** _____ to the alley, Bert paused and stared into the darkness.

5. "You can come out now, Detective Sardelli. I know you're in there!" **exclaimed** _____ Bert.

6. Detective Sardelli **languidly** _____ stepped forward into the light of the street with his hands above his head.

7. Suddenly, lights went on and there was cheering. "Surprise! Happy Birthday, Sardelli! We **deceived** _____ you, and it wasn't easy!"

Painting Pictures With Words

Authors use figurative language to describe things in a more vivid way. This helps the reader picture a particular scene more clearly. Example: The field of daffodils looked like a yellow blanket covering the earth.

Read each figurative sentence. Answer the questions.

1. Her eyes were as big as saucers.

   What two things are being compared? _____
   What picture do you see in your mind?

   _____

2. He raced down the track like lightning.

   What two things are being compared? _____
   What picture do you see in your mind?

   _____

3. The wounded dove rested in the protective arms of the tree.

   What two things are being compared? _____
   What picture do you see in your mind?

   _____

4. His heart pounded like a carpenter's hammer.

   What two things are being compared? _____
   What picture do you see in your mind?

   _____

That's a Fact!

A **fact** is a statement that can be proved. (Example: Dogs are furry mammals.)
An **opinion** is a statement expressing a belief, idea, or feeling that cannot be proved. (Example: Big dogs are more beautiful than small dogs.)

Read the following sentences. Write **F** on the line before the sentence if a fact is stated. Write **O** if an opinion is being given. Underline the word or words that are clues that an opinion is being given.

_____ 1. The White House is the office and home of the President and his family.

_____ 2. The White House is the most beautiful building in the U.S.A.

_____ 3. The Washington Monument is not as nice of a tribute to George Washington as the Lincoln Memorial is to Abraham Lincoln.

_____ 4. Seeing the cherry blossoms in bloom along the Potomac is an unforgettable sight to every Washington tourist in the spring.

_____ 5. The Smithsonian Institution is located in Washington, D.C.

_____ 6. San Francisco is built on and around more than 40 hills.

_____ 7. San Francisco's cable cars run on rails.

_____ 8. San Francisco is more beautiful than any other city.

_____ 9. The San Francisco Giants of the National League play baseball in Candlestick Park.

Is It the Real Thing?

> **Realistic fiction** has characters that are involved in events that could actually happen.

> **Fantasy** is fiction that contains settings, characters, or events that could not exist. However, it may contain some realistic features.

Read each paragraph. Write **R** on the line before the paragraph if it is realistic fiction. Write **F** if the paragraph is fantasy. In the paragraphs you label fantasy, underline the sentences that make them a fantasy.

_____ 1. Derek looked at the mountain. It was incredibly high. Could he reach its summit before sundown? He took a sip of water and began the slow journey.

_____ 2. Georgine sat alone in the examining room. She hated getting shots, and she knew one was coming. She started to cry. "Don't do that!" said a voice from the calendar on the wall. "Help me down from here. I've been hanging here for a whole month, and you think you've got problems!"

_____ 3. Carla was nervous. And whenever she was nervous, she either whistled or talked to herself. Today she talked to herself. "You know you can do this. You've practiced for days. You know your lines perfectly. Now get out there and WOW them!"

_____ 4. The elephant raised her trunk and squirted a mouthful of water into her mouth. Then she lowered her trunk into the river and refilled it. She repeated this process several times. Then she said, "Okay, Junior, now you try. It's really very easy. Practice makes perfect, and don't worry if you dribble."

It's the Proper Thing to Do!

Common nouns name people, places, and things.
   Example: girl, city, dog

Proper nouns name specific people, places, and things. Proper nouns begin with a capital letter.
   Example: Kendra, Saint-Tropez, Great Dane

Underline the common nouns and circle the proper nouns.

1. Jon changed the tire on the Chevrolet.

2. Allison asked for a map of St. Louis.

3. Queen Elizabeth dined at Buckingham Palace.

4. Eli's favorite ice cream is Häagen-Daz.

5. The dog tracked mud all over the kitchen floor.

6. The boys ate lunch at Denny's.

7. Harvey and Maria rode on the roller coaster at Magic Mountain.

8. My family went to Yellowstone National Park on vacation last year.

9. Some people rode down the Mississippi River in their rowboat.

10. Many people visit the Empire State Building in New York City.

A Bucket of Plurals

A **singular noun** names one person, place, or thing.

A **plural noun** names more than one person, place, or thing.

To make most singular nouns plural, add **s**.

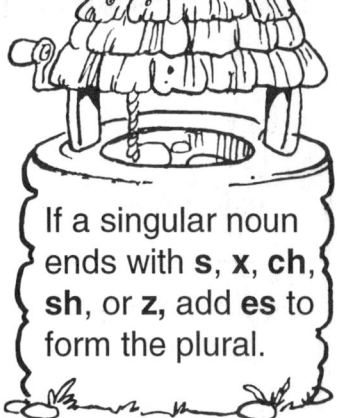

If a singular noun ends with **s**, **x**, **ch**, **sh**, or **z**, add **es** to form the plural.

Write the plural of each noun on the correct bucket.

class	ax	car	robot
desk	lamp	eraser	dress
brush	stick	peach	
buzz	bus	cave	

Added **s**

Added **es**

Possessive Rules

A **possessive noun** is a noun that names *who* or *what* has something.

Rule 1	Rule 2	Rule 3
Add an apostrophe and s (**'s**) to show the possessive of most singular nouns. Example: a girl's dress	Add an apostrophe (**'**) to show the possessive of plural nouns that end with **s**. Example: two girls' dresses	Add an apostrophe and s (**'s**) to show the possessive of plural nouns that do not end with **s**. Example: the children's clothes

Look at each picture. Write a possessive phrase and a rule number for each.

1. Rule _____

2. Rule _____

3. Rule _____

4. Rule _____

5. Rule _____

6. Rule _____

There, Their, They're

There shows direction.

Example: The boy put the book **there**.

Their shows ownership.

Example: It's **their** tree house.

They're is a contraction for *they are*.

Example: **They're** going swimming.

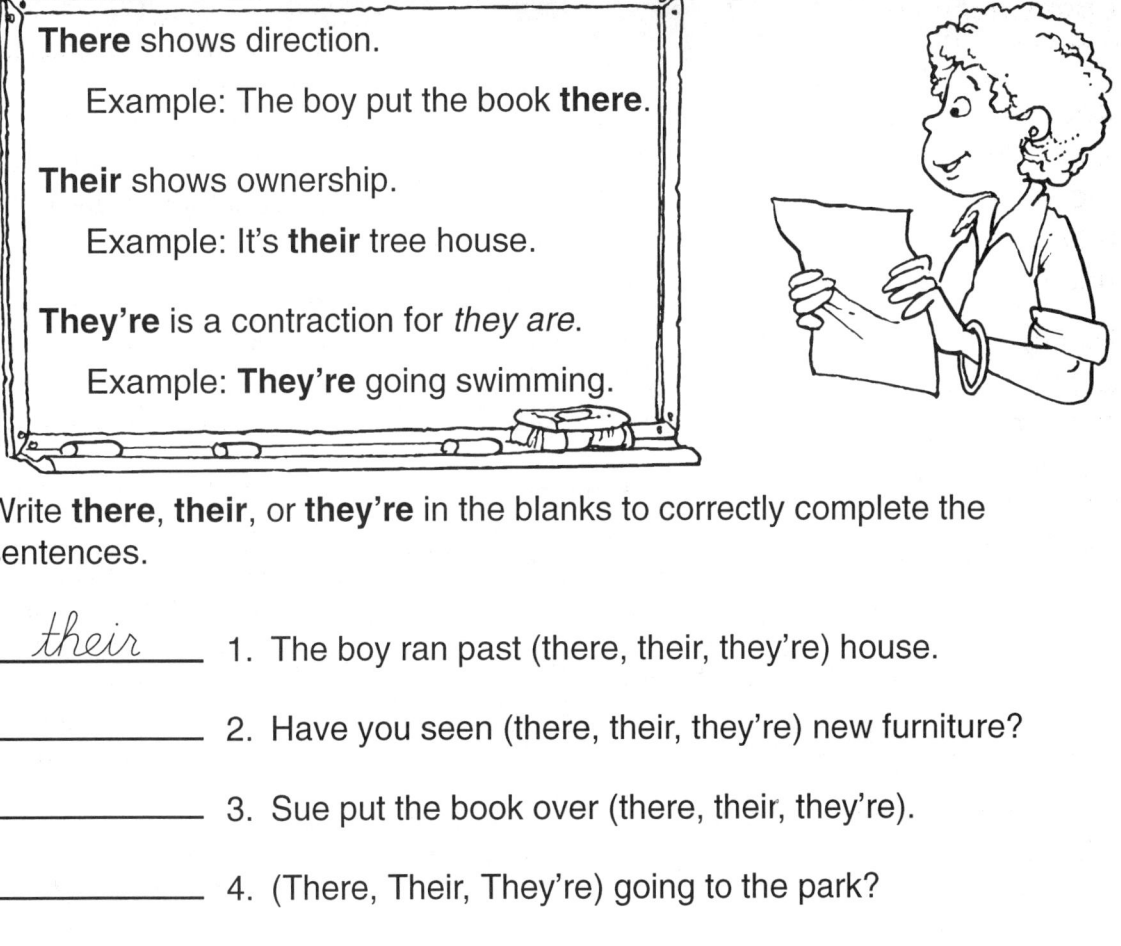

Write **there**, **their**, or **they're** in the blanks to correctly complete the sentences.

*their*_____ 1. The boy ran past (there, their, they're) house.

_____ 2. Have you seen (there, their, they're) new furniture?

_____ 3. Sue put the book over (there, their, they're).

_____ 4. (There, Their, They're) going to the park?

_____ 5. She is (there, their, they're) grandmother.

_____ 6. I could not go over (there, their, they're) until nine o'clock.

_____ 7. Do you think (there, their, they're) old or new shoes?

_____ 8. Is that (there, their, they're) boat in the water?

_____ 9. (There, Their, They're) having a birthday party.

_____ 10. Look over (there, their, they're)!

Past, Present, Future

Verbs have different forms to show whether something is happening right now (present tense), has already happened (past tense), or will happen (future tense).

Example: I **jump**. (present tense)
                I **jumped**. (past tense)
                I **will jump**. (future tense)

Underline the verb in each sentence. Then write whether each verb is in the **present**, **past**, or **future**.

_____ 1. My brother works in the tallest building in the city.

_____ 2. The baseball game starts in one hour.

_____ 3. My older sister talked on the phone for three hours.

_____ 4. The band will play at nine o'clock.

_____ 5. Tina vacuumed the living room floor.

_____ 6. We will hike through the mountains.

Complete the chart. Write the correct verb tense. The first one has been done for you.

Present	Past	Future
pass	passed	will pass
entertain		
		will remember
	cheered	

© Frank Schaffer Publications, Inc.   FS-11011 Fifth Grade Activities

From Healthy Roots, Big Words Grow!

A **prefix** is one or more letters added to the beginning of a root word. A prefix changes the meaning of the root word.

Prefix	Meaning	Example
mis	poorly, in the wrong way	misread (reads in the wrong way)
re	again	rewrite (write again)
in, un, dis	not, the opposite of	indestructible (not destructible)
pre	before	preview (view before)

Look at the words on the flower. Add a prefix from the box above to each word and write the word in one of the following sentences.

1. The lawyer was _____ in the argument.

2. Mia was _____ to the store clerk.

3. The coach _____ the rules to Olga.

4. Lee _____ the new player.

Flower words: judges, persuasive, considerate, states

In each sentence underline the word that has a prefix. Then write the meaning of the word.

5. The janitor <u>unlocks</u> the office door. *the opposite of locks*

6. The accountant mismanaged Sara's money. _____

7. Manuel was disrespectful toward his parents. _____

8. Stephen misplays part of the song. _____

9. Laura looks for an inexpensive restaurant. _____

Punctuation Station

A **comma** can be used to separate each item in a series of three or more nouns or verbs.

Example: The boy hopped, skipped, and jumped.

A **comma** can be used to set off the name of a person who is spoken to directly in a sentence.

Example: Tom, did you do your homework?

Write commas where they belong in the following sentences.

1. Speed skating figure skating and bobsledding are popular winter sports.

2. The children had cake milk sandwiches and apples for lunch.

3. Roberto needed to buy a bat a hat and a baseball glove.

4. Beverly I need a needle so I can sew this button on.

5. Mother may I go to the store to buy some candy?

6. Tara I really enjoyed reading your report about penguins.

7. Brian do you know who has my favorite eraser?

8. At the zoo, the family stopped and looked smiled and laughed at the monkeys.

9. Natalie do you think Keri Debi and Ken will come to the class picnic?

10. The fans at the football game cheered clapped and danced when their team made a touchdown.

How Interesting!

You can make sentences more interesting by using descriptive words that tell *what kind* of people, places, or things you are writing about.

Write two descriptive words on each blank below to make the sentences more interesting.

1. The _____*hungry, frisky*_____ hamster ate the paper towel.

2. Deb's _____ garden is now blooming.

3. Freddy told a _____ joke that made me laugh.

4. The _____ puppy wagged its tail when the girl rubbed his head.

5. Did you hear the _____ airplane flying above?

6. We ate _____ hamburgers at the picnic.

7. Our neighbor made _____ brownies for us.

8. The _____ bus stopped behind the blue convertible.

9. We drove past the _____ ocean on our way to Grandma's house.

10. The _____ babies are sleeping soundly.

11. Did you see my _____ jacket anywhere?

12. I left my _____ book at the library.

13. The _____ clouds are invisible today.

© Frank Schaffer Publications, Inc.   15   FS-11011 Fifth Grade Activities

Using Joining Words

You can combine sentences using these words: *and, but, or, because,* and *so.*

Examples: I need to brush my teeth. I am going to bed.
I need to brush my teeth *because* I am going to bed.

My brother likes broccoli. I do not like it.
My brother likes broccoli, *but* I do not like it.

Choose the best word to use from the word box and combine the pairs of sentences.

and	but	or	so	because

1. I like Henry. He always lends a helping hand.

   _____

   _____

2. Should I play basketball? Should I play baseball?

   _____

   _____

3. I want to go to the party. My mom said I may not go.

   _____

   _____

4. I was very tired. I took a little nap.

   _____

   _____

5. I answered the door. I heard the doorbell ring.

   _____

   _____

The Details, Please

A **paragraph** is made up of a topic sentence, supporting details, and a conclusion.
The **topic sentence** tells what the paragraph is about.
The **details** prove, explain, or support the topic sentence.
The **conclusion** restates the topic sentence.

Write two details for each topic sentence and conclusion below.

1. You can do many things to clean up the environment.

    * _____

    * _____

    Everyone can do something to clean the environment.

2. It is important to get enough sleep each day.

    * _____

    * _____

    Sleep is important for everyone.

3. There are many things children can do to help their parents.

    * _____

    * _____

    Children can be a big help to their parents.

Food for Thought

A **descriptive paragraph** describes something in detail. It creates a visual image with words.

Answer these questions about your favorite food. Use descriptive words in your answers.

How does it look? _____

How does it taste? _____

How does it smell? _____

What sound does it make when you eat it? _____
_____

How does it make you feel when you eat it? _____
_____

Now write a paragraph using the ideas you wrote above.

_____
_____
_____
_____
_____
_____
_____
_____

Imagine That!

Think of someone famous that you would like to meet. Pretend that you could spend the day with that person. Use your imagination and answer the questions below.

Who would you spend the day with? _____

What would you do? _____
_____

What might you talk about? _____
_____

How would you feel? _____
_____

Now write a story using the ideas you wrote above.

_____
_____
_____
_____
_____
_____
_____
_____
_____

Clear Directions

Informative writing presents basic information clearly.

If you are writing directions, you need to be sure that the person who reads the directions can follow them.

Write clear directions for the situations below.
You may want to use order words such as **first, then, next,** and **finally.**

How to Tie Your Shoelaces

How to Get From Your Classroom to the Library

Your Opinion Counts

The purpose of **expository writing** is to explain, state opinions, and persuade. Think about the questions below.

Who do you think has an important job?
Why do you think this job is important?

Write an expository paragraph that gives your opinions. Include at least five reasons for your choice.

An Important Job

_____
_____
_____
_____
_____
_____
_____
_____
_____
_____
_____
_____
_____
_____

Picasso

A time line presents important events and their dates in chronological order. Look at the time line outlining important events in the life of Pablo Picasso. Use this time line to answer each question.

```
1881        1901        1904        1908        1912        1937        1973
 |           |           |           |           |           |           |
born in                Rose Period              begins to use           dies in
Málaga,                begins—paints a lot      newspaper               France
Spain                  of circus scenes and     clippings in
                       uses warmer colors       his art

            Blue Period              begins to               creates painting
            begins—Picasso           paint in a              Guernica, showing
            paints with lots of      style known             the destruction of the
            blue                     as cubism               village by General
                                                             Franco during the
                                                             Spanish Civil War
```

1. How old was Picasso when he painted *Guernica*? _____

2. In what year did Picasso die? _____

3. Where was Picasso born? _____

4. When did Picasso begin to paint circus scenes? _____

5. How many years did Picasso's Blue Period last? _____

6. Did the Blue Period begin before or after 1912? _____

7. In what year did Picasso begin to paint in a style known as cubism? _____

Camp Meadows

At Camp Meadows, the camp director made a chart showing the number of children who participated in each activity for one month. Use the information on this chart to answer each question.

Activities	Week 1	Week 2	Week 3
Swimming	300	200	620
Sailing	250	530	340
Kayaking	123	264	93
Arts and Crafts	302	105	54
Horseback Riding	179	245	195
Hiking	216	154	100
Fishing	50	264	62

1. What was the most popular activity during week 2? _____

2. How many children went fishing during week 3? _____

3. Did more children go kayaking or hiking during week 1? _____

4. What was the least popular activity during week 1? _____

5. How many more children went sailing than hiking during week 2? _____

6. How many children went horseback riding altogether? _____

7. During week 2, which two activities had an equal number of children participating in them? _____

© Frank Schaffer Publications, Inc.   23   FS-11011 Fifth Grade Activities

Directions

The compass rose on this map shows the directions north (N), south (S), east (E), and west (W). There are also divisions for the intermediate directions—northeast, southeast, southwest, and northwest. Use this map to answer each question.

1. Start in Washington. Move south one state, southeast one state, and east one state. Where are you? _____

2. Start in Texas. Move north two states, east one state, and northeast one state. Where are you? _____

3. After moving north one state, northeast one state, and southeast one state, you are in Missouri. Where did you start? _____

4. Start in South Carolina. Move southwest one state, west two states, northwest one state, and west one state. Where are you? _____

Flowers

The Wilson family made this picture graph to show the number of flowers they planted. Use the picture graph to answer each question.

Number of Flowers Planted

Morning Glory	❀ ❀ ❀ ❀ ❀ ❀ ❀
Rose	❀ ❀ ❀ ❀ ❀ ✿
Tulip	❀ ❀ ❀ ✿
Daffodil	❀ ❀ ❀ ❀ ❀ ❀
Pansy	❀ ❀
Marigold	❀ ❀ ❀ ❀ ❀ ❀ ❀ ❀ ✿

❀ represents 10 flowers

1. How many morning glories were planted? _____
2. What kind of flower was planted the most? _____
3. What kind of flower was planted the least? _____
4. How many tulips were planted? _____
5. How many more roses were planted than pansies? _____
6. Were there more roses or daffodils planted? _____
7. How many fewer morning glories were planted than marigolds? _____
8. How many more daffodils were planted than tulips? _____

A Graph of Rivers

A bar graph can be used to compare information. The bar graph below shows information about the lengths of famous rivers. Use the bar graph to answer each question.

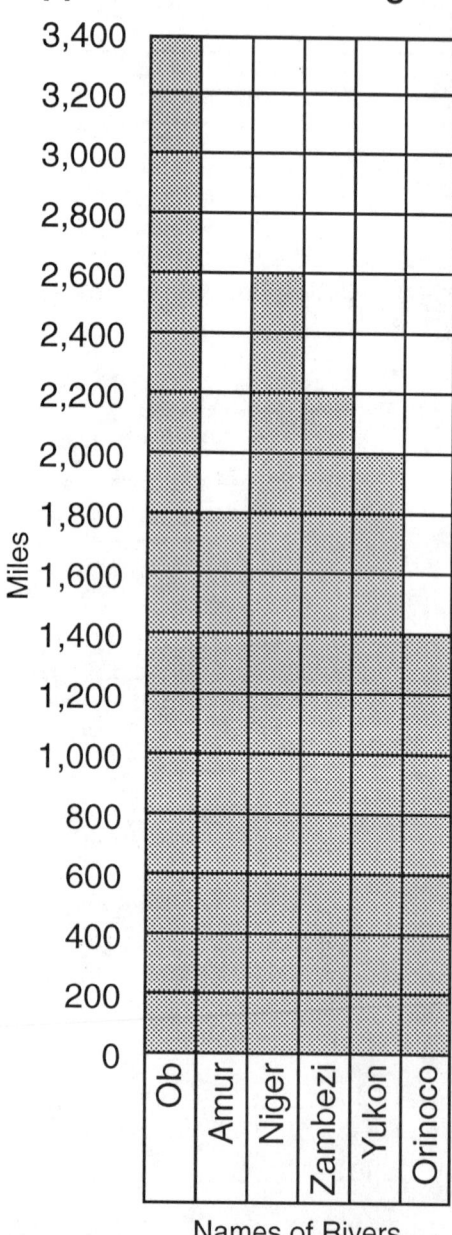

1. How many more miles is the Ob River than the Niger River? _____

2. How many miles long is the Yukon River? _____

3. How many fewer miles is the Orinoco River than the Amur River? _____

4. What is the name of the longest river on this graph? _____

5. Which river is 1,800 miles long?
   _____

6. What is the name of the shortest river on this graph? _____

7. How many more miles is the Zambezi River than the Orinoco River? _____

8. If the Yukon River were 400 miles longer, how long would it be? _____

Pull-Out Answers

Page 1
4–To warm up . . .
6–Then he joined . . .
3–On the day of the race, . . .
1–First, Mark signed up . . .
7–Finally, a horn blared . . .
5–After the jog, . . .
2–Next, to train for the . . .

5–Soon the day . . .
1–First, April and Lisa . . .
4–Then they looked . . .
7–Finally, they drove to . . .
2–Next, they called . . .
6–They packed . . .
3–They received . . .

Page 2
1. Thomas Edison was one of the greatest inventors.
2. There are many interesting facts about Saturn.

Page 3
1. The largest part . . .
   Shrimp have five . . .
   Shrimp have long, . . .
2. The sea horse's shape . . .
   The sea horse swims . . .
   It is covered . . .
3. The arms help . . .
   The starfish can regrow . . .
   Under each arm, . . .

Page 4
1. A
2. D
3. E
4. C
5. F
6. B
7. G

Page 5
Accept reasonable answers for descriptions. Possible answers listed below.
1. eyes, saucers
   a girl/woman with very large eyes
2. how he ran, speed of lightning
   a boy/man running very quickly
3. arms, tree branches
   dove resting in tree branches
4. heart, hammer
   a boy/man in a panic

Page 6
1. F
2. O–most beautiful
3. O–not as nice
4. O–an unforgettable sight
5. F
6. F
7. F
8. O–more beautiful
9. F

Page 7
1. R
2. F–"Don't do that!" said a voice from the calendar on the wall. "Help me down from here. I've been hanging here for a whole month, and you think you've got problems!"
3. R
4. F–Then she said, "okay, Junior, now you try. It's really very easy. Practice makes perfect, and don't worry if you dribble."

Page 8
Common nouns are underlined and proper nouns are boldfaced.
1. **Jon** changed the tire on the **Chevrolet**.
2. **Allison** asked for a map of **St. Louis**.
3. **Queen Elizabeth** dined at **Buckingham Palace**.
4. **Eli's** favorite ice cream is **Häagen-Daz**.
5. The dog tracked mud all over the kitchen floor.
6. The boys ate lunch at **Denny's**.
7. **Harvey** and **Maria** rode on the roller coaster at **Magic Mountain**.
8. My family went to **Yellowstone National Park** on vacation last year.
9. Some people rode down the **Mississippi River** in their rowboat.
10. Many people visit the **Empire State Building** in **New York City**.

Page 9
Added **s**
cars
robots
desks
lamps
erasers
sticks
caves

Added **es**
classes
axes
dresses
brushes
peaches
buzzes
buses

Pull-Out Answers

Page 10
1. Rule **1**—the boy's bike
2. Rule **2**—the dogs' bones
3. Rule **2**—the birds' nests
4. Rule **1**—the mouse's cheese
5. Rule **2**—the farmers' tractors
6. Rule **3**—the men's hats

Page 11
1. their
2. their
3. there
4. They're
5. their
6. there
7. they're
8. their
9. They're
10. there

Page 12
1. present—<u>works</u>
2. present—<u>starts</u>
3. past—<u>talked</u>
4. future—<u>will play</u>
5. past—<u>vacuumed</u>
6. future—<u>will hike</u>

entertained, will entertain
remember, remembered
cheer, will cheer

Page 13
1. unpersuasive
2. inconsiderate
3. restates or misstates
4. misjudges or prejudges
5. unlocks—the opposite of locks
6. mismanaged—poorly managed
7. disrespectful—not respectful
8. misplays—plays in the wrong way
9. inexpensive—not expensive

Page 14
1. Speed skating**,** figure skating**,** and bobsledding are popular winter sports.
2. The children had cake**,** milk**,** sandwiches**,** and apples for lunch.
3. Roberto needed to buy a bat**,** a hat**,** and a baseball glove.
4. Beverly**,** I need a needle so I can sew this button on.
5. Mother**,** may I go to the store to buy some candy?
6. Tara**,** I really enjoyed reading your report about penguins.
7. Brian**,** do you know who has my favorite eraser?
8. At the zoo**,** the family stopped and looked**,** smiled**,** and laughed at the monkeys.
9. Natalie**,** do you think Keri**,** Debi**,** and Ken will come to the class picnic?
10. The fans at the football game cheered**,** clapped**,** and danced when their team made a touchdown.

Page 15
Answers will vary. Page completed according to directions.

Page 16
1. I like Henry **because** he always lends a helping hand.
2. Should I play basketball**, or** should I play baseball?
3. I want to go to the party**, but** my mom said I may not go.
4. I was very tired**, so** I took a little nap.
5. I answered the door **because** I heard the doorbell ring.

Page 17
Answers will vary. Page completed according to directions.

Page 18
Answers will vary. Paragraphs will vary.

Page 19
Answers will vary. Stories will vary.

Page 20
Directions will vary.

Page 21
Paragraphs will vary, but should include at least five reasons.

Page 22
1. 56 years old
2. 1973
3. Málaga, Spain
4. 1904
5. 3 years
6. before
7. 1908

Page 23
1. sailing
2. 62
3. hiking
4. fishing
5. 376
6. 619
7. kayaking and fishing

© Frank Schaffer Publications, Inc.

FS-11011 Fifth Grade Activities

Pull-Out Answers

Page 24
1. Utah
2. Illinois
3. New Mexico
4. Oklahoma

Page 25
1. 70
2. marigold
3. pansy
4. 35
5. 35
6. daffodils
7. 15
8. 25

Page 26
1. 800 miles
2. 2,000 miles
3. 400 miles
4. Ob River
5. Amur River
6. Orinoco River
7. 800 miles
8. 2,400 miles

Page 27
1. Monday
2. Sunday
3. 44
4. 18
5. Wednesday
6. Thursday
7. Wednesday and Thursday

Page 28
1. false
2. true
3. false
4. true
5. false
6. true

Page 29
D–611; I–756; H–967; A–357
S–6,723; T–7,168; G–8,468; E–5,232
W–46,864; C–781,782; Y–484,903; N–55,863
M–517; F–817; O–746; U–1,438
IT WAS NICE GNAWING YOU!

Page 30
R–160; T–3,111; L–1,511; D–263
A–5,208; I–4,175; U–7,073; G–89,191
M–8,246; S–250,165; H–99,397; J–239,019
E–11,005; C–27,309; O–534,532; K–15,660
A STRAIGHT RULER!

Page 31

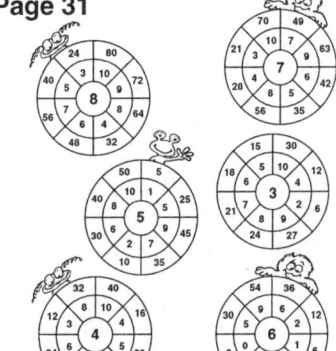

Page 32
A. 172, 480, 85, 198
B. 108, 261, 392, 224, 162
C. 192, 225, 215, 106, 256, 340
D. 546, 588, 48, 693, 182, 290
E. 261, 768, 78, 651, 312, 120
F. 207, 170, 171, 738, 260, 332

Page 33
E–1,095; A–1,804; U–5,292; R–4,320
J–48,616; M–1,776; F–1,392; O–22,692
I–31,038; P–1,724; N–2,835; K–16,824
H–1,467; C–14,224; T–7,902; D–20,868
THE TEMPERATURE

Page 34
A. 775; 1,748; 1,848; 2,030
B. 1,792; 2,997; 1,752; 3,825
C. 891; 1,156; 1,998; 4,018
D. 5,124; 2,728; 2,301

Page 35
A. 6, 7, 8
B. 7, 9, 6
C. 7, 9, 4
D. 5, 8, 4, 6, 9
E. 9, 4, 6, 5, 3
F. 7, 9, 4, 5, 3
G. 2, 9, 5, 9, 8
H. 0, 6, 5
I. 7, 6, 8
J. 3, 6, 3
K. 7, 6, 7

Page 36
C–5 R7; P–5 R3; I–4 R4; N–9 R1

K–8 R3; T–9 R2; U–5 R2; M–9 R3

O–2 R3; Y–3 R3; E–3 R4; L–4 R1

MOUNT MCKINLEY

Page 37
T–248 R1; R–147 R4; I–339; N–61 R5

L–156 R3; H–443 R4; E–233; V–123 R6

THE NILE RIVER

Page 38
A. 602 R1; 806 R4; 402 R2
B. 906 R1; 20 R3; 205
C. 901 R1; 109 R5; 700 R2

© Frank Schaffer Publications, Inc.

Pull-Out Answers

Page 39
1. yes
2. no
3. yes
4. no
5. yes
6. yes
7. yes
8. yes
9. no
10. yes
11. yes
12. no
13. yes
14. yes
15. yes

Page 40
1. Vol. 19 for Typewriter
2. Vol. 8 for Gem,
   Vol. 1 for Aquamarine
3. Vol. 13 for Music,
   Vol. 19 for Trumpet
4. Vol. 18 for Solar System
5. Vol. 14 for Olympic Games
6. Vol. 18 for Socrates,
   Vol. 15 for Philosophy

Page 41
The following words should be circled under the guide words.

rank   rasp
   rarity
   rapacious
   ransom
   rash

Pompeii   popcorn
   poor
   ponder
   poodle
   ponderous

entree   epidermis
   epidemic
   envelope
   entrench
   envious

gallery   gargle
   garage
   gardenia
   gamble
   galoshes
   garbage
   gallows

Page 42
1. **2**
2. **3**
3. **9**
4. **5**
5. **2**
6. **6**
7. **7**
8. **4**
9. **5**
10. **5**
11. **1**
12. **8**
13. **7**

Page 43
1. p
2. i
3. l
4. o
5. m
6. n
7. h
8. e
9. k
10. f
11. c
12. j
13. d
14. g
15. b
16. a

Page 44
Learn Golf in a Day 700–799
Guitar for Beginners 700–799
Easy Science Experiments 500–599
Ancient Philosophy 100–199
Greek Mythology 200–299
New Children's Dictionary 400–499
Chinese Customs 300–399
Our Solar System 500–599
Modern Medicine 600–699
Keeping Your Garden Green 600–699
Favorite Fairy Tales 300–399
Summer Sports 700–799
Watercolor Painting 700–799
Beginning Chemistry 500–599
Learning Spanish 400–499
Animal Encyclopedia 000–099

Page 45
   Ants are amazing weightlifters**.** **T**hey can lift things that **weigh** 50 times more **than** they do. Have you seen them carry **h**uge leaves**,** twigs**,** and dead insects across the lawn**?** If you compared their si**z**e to the things they carry, you'd **be** amazed.

Page 46
Answers will vary. Page completed according to directions.

Page 47
1. b, c
2. a, b
3. a, b, c
4. a, c
5. a, b, c

Page 48
Answers will vary. Page completed according to directions.

Page 49
Answers will vary. Page completed according to directions.

Page 50
Answers will vary. Page completed according to directions.

Page 51
Supporting answers will vary.
1. Kaitlin
2. Tanesha
3. Sandy

Page 52
Explanations will vary.
1. Sarah and Tim ran into the kitchen, . . .
2. The man got a ladder.

Talk! Talk! Talk!

A line graph can show changes over time. Line segments on the graph can move up, move down, or stay the same. This graph shows how many phone calls the Spino family made in a week. Use the graph to answer each question.

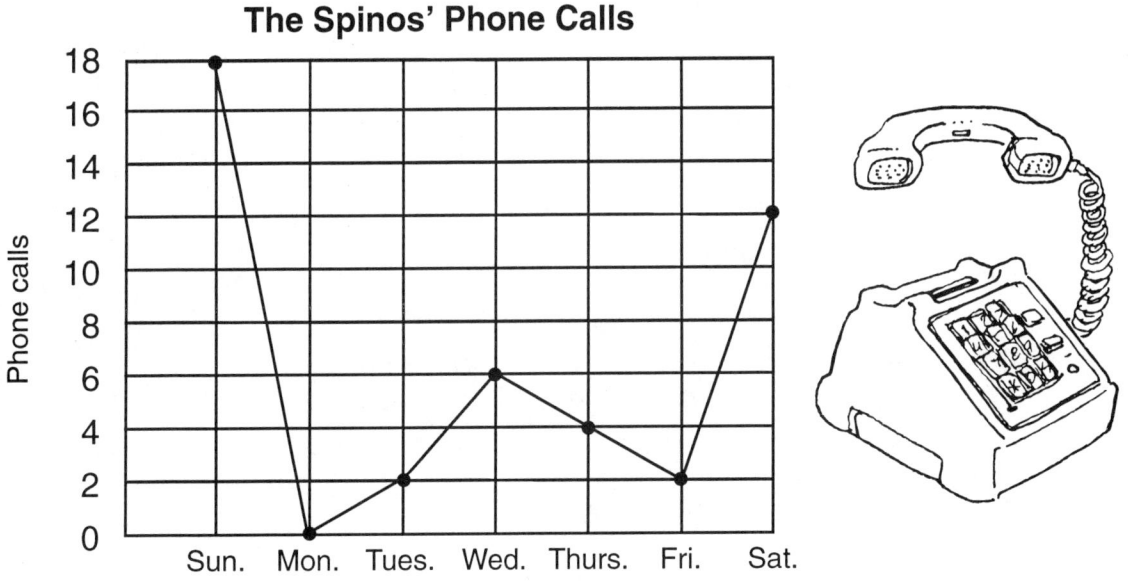

1. On which day were no phone calls made? _____
2. On which day were the most phone calls made? _____
3. What was the total number of phone calls for the entire week? _____
4. What was the greatest number of phone calls made in one day? _____
5. On which day did the Spino family make six phone calls? _____
6. Were more phone calls made on Tuesday or Thursday? _____
7. On which two days did they make 10 phone calls altogether?

_____

Scrumptious Pies

A circle graph is a circle divided into parts that display information.

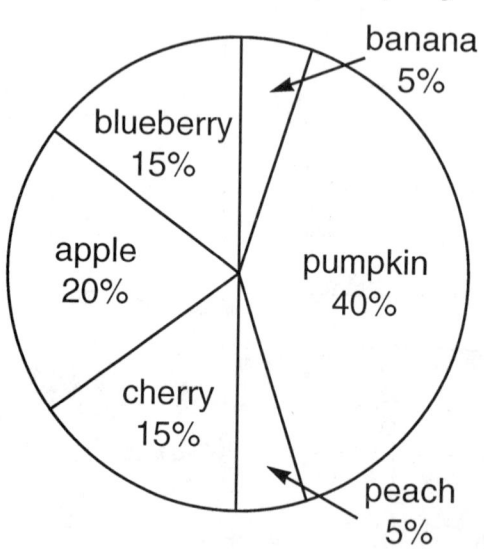

Pies Made by the Scrumptious Pie Company

Use the circle graph to answer each question. Write **true** or **false** below.

_____ 1. Scrumptious makes more blueberry pies than apple pies.

_____ 2. Scrumptious makes fewer peach pies than cherry pies.

_____ 3. Peach and banana pies represent about $\frac{1}{3}$ of the pies made at Scrumptious.

_____ 4. Scrumptious makes fewer apple pies than pumpkin pies.

_____ 5. Scrumptious makes more banana pies than peach pies.

_____ 6. Scrumptious makes more apple and cherry pies than blueberry and banana pies.

© Frank Schaffer Publications, Inc.   28   FS-11011 Fifth Grade Activities

Riddle Me With Addition

Add.

D 532 + 79	**I** 681 + 75	**H** 641 + 326	**A** 322 + 35
S 4,356 + 2,367	**T** 6,578 + 590	**G** 3,478 + 4,990	**E** 4,635 + 597
W 39,189 + 7,675	**C** 562,037 + 219,745	**Y** 457,663 + 27,240	**N** 23,742 + 32,121
M 128 357 + 32	**F** 454 29 + 334	**O** 332 176 + 238	**U** 543 126 + 769

Fill in the correct letter over each answer. What did the beaver say to the tree?

___ ___ ___ ___ ___ ___ ___ ___ ___
756 7,168 46,864 357 6,723 55,863 756 781,782 5,232

___ ___ ___ ___ ___ ___ ___ ___ ___ ___ !
8,468 55,863 357 46,864 756 55,863 8,468 484,903 746 1,438

A King's Ransom

Subtract.

R 395 − 235	T 8,769 − 5,658	L 2,316 − 805	D 362 − 99
A 7,636 − 2,428	I 15,767 − 11,592	U 20,707 − 13,634	G 172,359 − 83,168
M 14,479 − 6,233	S 479,100 − 228,935	H 999,106 − 899,709	J 276,317 − 37,298
E 500,030 − 489,025	C 70,038 − 42,729	O 768,987 − 234,455	K 23,554 − 7,894

Fill in the correct letter over each answer. What is an honest king called?

___ ___ ___ ___ ___ ___ ___ ___ ___
5,208 250,165 3,111 160 5,208 4,175 89,191 99,397 3,111

___ ___ ___ ___ ___ !
160 7,073 1,511 11,005 160

Multiplication Wheels

Multiply to complete the multiplication wheels.

Wheel 1 (center 8): 40, 3, 10, 9, 8, 4, 6, 7 (outer: 5); inner ring values 5, 3, 10, 9, 8, 4, 6, 7

Wheel 2 (center 7): 10, 7, 9, 6, 5, 8, 4, 3

Wheel 3 (center 5): 10, 1, 5, 9, 7, 2, 6, 8

Wheel 4 (center 3): 5, 10, 4, 2, 9, 8, 7, 6

Wheel 5 (center 4): 8, 10, 4, 5, 7, 9, 6, 3

Wheel 6 (center 6): 9, 6, 2, 1, 8, 10, 0, 5

31   FS-11011 Fifth Grade Activities

© Frank Schaffer Publications, Inc.

Abracadabra!

Multiply.

A.
```
  1
 43      60      17      33
× 4     × 8     × 5     × 6
---     ---     ---     ---
172
```

B.
```
 36      29      49      32      18
× 3     × 9     × 8     × 7     × 9
---     ---     ---     ---     ---
```

C.
```
 24      75      43      53      64      85
× 8     × 3     × 5     × 2     × 4     × 4
---     ---     ---     ---     ---     ---
```

D.
```
 91      84      16      77      26      58
× 6     × 7     × 3     × 9     × 7     × 5
---     ---     ---     ---     ---     ---
```

E.
```
 87      96      39      93      78      40
× 3     × 8     × 2     × 7     × 4     × 3
---     ---     ---     ---     ---     ---
```

F.
```
 23      34      57      82      52      83
× 9     × 5     × 3     × 9     × 5     × 4
---     ---     ---     ---     ---     ---
```

Riddle Me With Multiplication

Multiply.

E ¹¹365 × 3 1,095	A 451 × 4	U 756 × 7	R 864 × 5
J 6,077 × 8	M 592 × 3	F 174 × 8	O 5,673 × 4
I 5,173 × 6	P 431 × 4	N 567 × 5	K 2,804 × 6
H 163 × 9	C 7,112 × 2	T 878 × 9	D 3,478 × 6

Fill in the correct letter over each answer. What can you measure that has no length, width, or thickness?

___ ___ ___
7,902 1,467 1,095

___ ___ ___ ___ ___ ___ ___ ___ ___ ___ ___
7,902 1,095 1,776 1,724 1,095 4,320 1,804 7,902 5,292 4,320 1,095

Let's Multiply

Multiply.

A.
```
   31          38          56          70
 x 25        x 46        x 33        x 29
  155
  620
  775
```

B.
```
   56          81          24          51
 x 32        x 37        x 73        x 75
```

C.
```
   27          68          54          82
 x 33        x 17        x 37        x 49
```

D.
```
   61          88          59
 x 84        x 31        x 39
```

Division Goal!

Divide.

A. 7)̄42̄ (6)   5)̄35̄   7)̄56̄

B. 8)̄56̄   9)̄81̄   3)̄18̄

C. 3)̄21̄   3)̄27̄   9)̄36̄

D. 6)̄30̄   9)̄72̄   8)̄32̄   2)̄12̄   4)̄36̄

E. 5)̄45̄   4)̄16̄   6)̄36̄   7)̄35̄   6)̄18̄

F. 4)̄28̄   8)̄72̄   7)̄28̄   4)̄20̄   5)̄15̄

G. 9)̄18̄   6)̄54̄   5)̄25̄   2)̄18̄   3)̄24̄

H. 0 ÷ 4 = _____   48 ÷ 8 = _____   45 ÷ 9 = _____

I. 63 ÷ 9 = _____   54 ÷ 9 = _____   64 ÷ 8 = _____

J. 24 ÷ 8 = _____   24 ÷ 4 = _____   21 ÷ 7 = _____

K. 49 ÷ 7 = _____   30 ÷ 5 = _____   14 ÷ 2 = _____

As High As the Clouds

Divide.

C 8) 47 5 R7 40 7	P 7) 38	I 6) 28	N 4) 37
K 6) 51	T 3) 29	U 3) 17	M 4) 39
O 6) 15	Y 5) 18	E 7) 25	L 8) 33

Fill in the correct letter over each number. What is the tallest mountain in North America?

___ ___ ___ ___ ___
9 R3 2 R3 5 R2 9 R1 9 R2

___ ___ ___ ___ ___ ___ ___ ___
9 R3 5 R7 8 R3 4 R4 9 R1 4 R1 3 R4 3 R3

Down by the River

Divide.

T	R	I	N
$$\begin{array}{r}248\text{ R}1\\3\overline{)745}\\\underline{6}\\14\\\underline{12}\\25\\\underline{24}\\1\end{array}$$	$5\overline{)739}$	$6\overline{)2{,}034}$	$8\overline{)493}$
L	**H**	**E**	**V**
$6\overline{)939}$	$7\overline{)3{,}105}$	$4\overline{)932}$	$8\overline{)990}$

Fill in the correct letter over each answer. What is the longest river in the world?

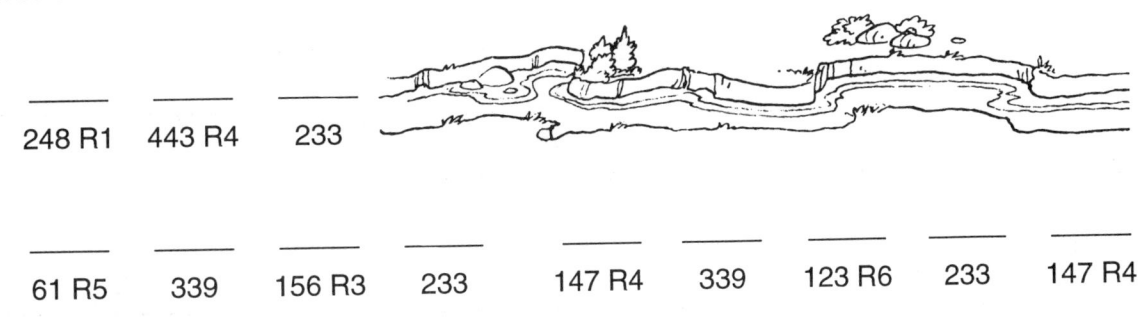

___   ___   ___
248 R1   443 R4   233

___   ___   ___   ___   ___   ___   ___   ___
61 R5   339   156 R3   233   147 R4   339   123 R6   233   147 R4

© Frank Schaffer Publications, Inc. 37 FS-11011 Fifth Grade Activities

A Flock of Problems

Divide.

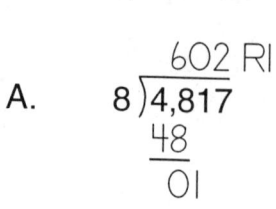

A.
```
       602 R1
    8)4,817
      48
      ‾‾
       01
        0
        ‾
        17
        16
        ‾‾
         1
```

7)5,646

3)1,208

B.   4)3,625

7)143

2)410

C.   5)4,506

6)659

3)2,102

Useful Information

Encyclopedias provide facts. They give information about people, places, and things. You can find the answers to some of the questions below in an encyclopedia.

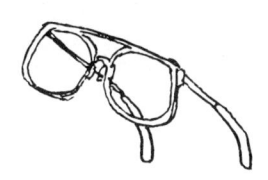

Circle **yes** or **no** to tell if you think an answer for the question can be found in an encyclopedia.

1. Who was Pablo Picasso?   yes   no
2. How do you pronounce *ukulele*?   yes   no
3. What is a tsunami?   yes   no
4. What will the weather be like this weekend?   yes   no
5. Who was the third president of the United States?   yes   no
6. What are two types of camels?   yes   no
7. How does an electric circuit work?   yes   no
8. What is the main product of Japan?   yes   no
9. How many students in your school wear glasses?   yes   no
10. What is a needleleaf tree?   yes   no
11. Where in Africa is Cameroon?   yes   no
12. Who is the most popular singer in your town?   yes   no
13. What are the different breeds of horses?   yes   no
14. What does a blue whale eat?   yes   no
15. Is a lobster a fish?   yes   no

Find the Answers

An **encyclopedia** provides information about important people, events, and general topics.

A	B	C-CH	CI-CZ	D	E	F	G	H	I	J-K	L	M	N-O	P	Q-R	S-SN	SO-SZ	T	U-V	WX YZ
1	2	3	4	5	6	7	8	9	10	11	12	13	14	15	16	17	18	19	20	21

If you want to find out what style of painting Pierre Auguste Renoir was best known for, you might look in Volume 16 for Renoir or in Volume 15 for Painting.

Fill in the circle next to each volume you could look in to find the answers to the questions.

1. Who invented the typewriter?

    ○ Vol. 19 for Typewriter   ○ Vol. 21 for Who

2. What type of gem is an aquamarine?

    ○ Vol. 8 for Gem   ○ Vol. 1 for Aquamarine

3. What type of musical instrument is a trumpet?

    ○ Vol. 13 for Music   ○ Vol. 19 for Trumpet

4. How many planets are in the Solar System?

    ○ Vol. 13 for Many   ○ Vol. 18 for Solar System

5. When did bicycle racing become an event at the Olympic Games?

    ○ Vol. 6 for Event   ○ Vol. 14 for Olympic Games

6. When did the Greek philosopher Socrates die?

    ○ Vol. 18 for Socrates   ○ Vol. 15 for Philosophy

Be My Guide

The **guide words** at the top of a dictionary page indicate the first and the last word on that page. All the other words on that page are listed in alphabetical order between the guide words.

Look at the guide words at the top of each sample page. Circle the words that could be found on each page.

rank rasp	Pompeii popcorn
rarity	pomp
rapacious	polo
rattle	portrait
range	poor
rather	pomade
ransom	ponder
racial	poodle
rash	ponderous

entree epidermis	gallery gargle
genius	garage
epidemic	gardenia
entomb	gamble
envelope	generally
entrench	galoshes
enter	garbage
elephant	gallows
envious	galleon

Many Meanings

The words listed alphabetically in a dictionary are called **entry words**. Most entries have several meanings for the same word.

> **run** (run) **v. 1.** To move the legs quickly, faster than walking. **2.** To go in a hurry. **3.** To flow. **4.** To be a candidate for election. **5.** To go, function, keep moving. **n. 6.** A quick trip. **7.** A unit of score in baseball. **8.** A series of regular performances. **9.** A place where stitches have become unraveled.

Each of the following sentences contains a form of the word *run*. Write the number of the definition that best fits the sentence.

_____ 1. Please **run** for help!

_____ 2. When the sap **runs**, it's time to collect the maple syrup.

_____ 3. Oh, no! I caught my stockings on a nail and got a **run** in them.

_____ 4. How does your car **run** since the tune-up?

_____ 5. I need to **run** to catch the bus.

_____ 6. Let's take a **run** over to the mall this evening.

_____ 7. Ben's team scored five **runs** in the sixth inning.

_____ 8. She is planning to **run** for governor next year.

_____ 9. The train **runs** from San Diego to San Francisco.

_____ 10. Does your watch **run** well or do you need a new one?

_____ 11. Which student in your class can **run** the fastest?

_____ 12. That play was not very popular. It had a very short **run**.

_____ 13. How many **runs** did your team score in the game?

Dictionary Pronunciations

Each word in a dictionary is given with its pronunciation. In pronunciations, letters of the alphabet and symbols are used to stand for sounds. A **pronunciation key** explains the symbols.

Match the following pronunciations by writing the letter of the correct spelling in the space provided. Use the pronunciation key to help you.

_____ 1. (ri lī´ əbəl)	a. persist
_____ 2. (steg´ ə sôr´ əs)	b. notably
_____ 3. (strid´n)	c. hostility
_____ 4. (stēp)	d. megaphone
_____ 5. (kən dens´)	e. denounce
_____ 6. (strēm´ līnd´)	f. conciliate
_____ 7. (strē´ mər)	g. notable
_____ 8. (di nouns´)	h. streamer
_____ 9. (den´ sətē)	i. stegosaurus
_____ 10. (kən sil´ ē āt)	j. department
_____ 11. (ho stil´ ə tē)	k. density
_____ 12. (di pärt´ mənt)	l. stridden
_____ 13. (meg´ ə fōn)	m. condense
_____ 14. (nō´ tə bəl)	n. streamlined
_____ 15. (nō´ tə blē)	o. steep
_____ 16. (pər sist´)	p. reliable

Pronunciation Key

a	bat
ā	ape
ä	are
e	get
ē	eat
ėr	fern
i	is
ī	ice
o	not
ō	over
ô	store
oi	oil
ou	out
u	fun
ů	put
ü	rule
ə	a in alone
	e in taken
	i in pencil
	o in melon
	u in virus

© Frank Schaffer Publications, Inc.   43   FS-11011 Fifth Grade Activities

Dewey Decimal System

The **Dewey Decimal System** puts books into categories, and each category has a number.

Numbers:	Category
000–099	General Works (reference books, encyclopedias)
100–199	Philosophy, Psychology
200–299	Religion, Myths
300–399	Social Sciences (folklore, fairy tales, law, political science, customs/holidays)
400–499	Languages, Dictionaries
500–599	Math, Science (astronomy, physics, chemistry, biology, botany, zoology)
600–699	Technology (medicine, engineering, gardening, home economics)
700–799	Arts (architecture, sculpture, drawing, painting, music, sports and recreation)

Write the Dewey Decimal category numbers after the titles below to show where these books would be shelved.

Learn Golf in a Day _____

Guitar for Beginners _____

Easy Science Experiments _____

Ancient Philosophy _____

Greek Mythology _____

New Children's Dictionary _____

Chinese Customs _____

Our Solar System _____

Modern Medicine _____

Keeping Your Garden Green _____

Favorite Fairy Tales _____

Summer Sports _____

Watercolor Painting _____

Beginning Chemistry _____

Learning Spanish _____

Animal Encyclopedia _____

Going Buggy

The story below has been proofread. Use the chart to find out what the symbols mean. Then rewrite the story correctly.

Symbol	Meaning
∧	Insert a letter, word, phrase, or sentence.
ℓ	Take out a letter, word, phrase, or sentence.
⊙	Insert a period.
/	Change a capital letter to a small letter.
≡	Change a small letter to a capital letter.
SP	Check the spelling of a word.
¶	Begin a new paragraph.

¶ Aunts (SP) are amazing weightlifters⊙ ≡they can lift things that way 50 times more then (SP) they do. Have you seen them carry ∧Huge leaves∧ twigs∧ and a̶n̶d̶ dead insects across the lawn∧ ≡if you compared their size to the things they carry, you'd bee̶ amazed.

_____

_____

_____

_____

_____

_____

Getting the Facts Straight

A **relevant fact** is information that a person needs to know in order to do the task.

An **irrelevant fact** is information that a person does not need to know in order to do the task.

Write one relevant fact and one irrelevant fact for each situation.

The Situation	Relevant Facts	Irrelevant Facts
1. planning a Valentine's Day party	where the party will be held	how many students have birthdays in February
2. getting tickets to a college basketball game		
3. setting up the new stereo system		

What Will They Do?

A story does not always tell you everything you want to know. Sometimes you have to make a guess based on known facts. This process is called making **inferences**.

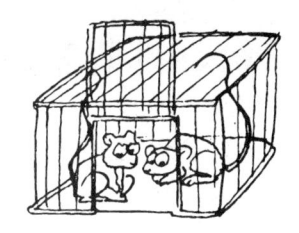

Read the sentences. Then underline the statements that are logical inferences.

1. Bernice and Andrew like to cook outdoors, go hiking, and watch sports.
   a. Bernice and Andrew will go to watch a play.
   b. Bernice and Andrew will go camping.
   c. Bernice and Andrew will go to a baseball game.

2. Heather and Todd enjoy studying about sea animals.
   a. Heather and Todd will go to the ocean and investigate sea life.
   b. Heather and Todd will watch a movie about dolphins.
   c. Heather and Todd will go out for a pizza.

3. Tina and Fernando enjoy growing their own food and being outdoors.
   a. Tina and Fernando will plant a garden.
   b. Tina and Fernando will go water skiing on the lake.
   c. Tina and Fernando will go horseback riding along the beach.

4. Lisa and Don enjoy listening to music, singing, and playing in the band.
   a. Lisa and Don will go to the symphony.
   b. Lisa and Don will have hamburgers for dinner.
   c. Lisa and Don will join the school choir.

5. Rosalie and Randall enjoy exercising. They enjoy eating Italian food.
   a. Rosalie and Randall will run a 10K race.
   b. Rosalie and Randall will go out for a spaghetti dinner.
   c. Rosalie and Randall will train for a triathlon.

Just Because!

The **cause** is the event that makes something happen.
The **effect** is the thing that happens, or the outcome.
Write a cause and an effect for each pair of pictures.

Cause		Effect
	Cause: _____ _____ _____ _____ Effect: _____ _____ _____ _____ _____	

Cause		Effect
	Cause: _____ _____ _____ _____ Effect: _____ _____ _____ _____ _____	

What's Wrong With This Picture?

Sometimes you must use the facts and your personal knowledge to draw a conclusion.

Use the picture to answer each question.

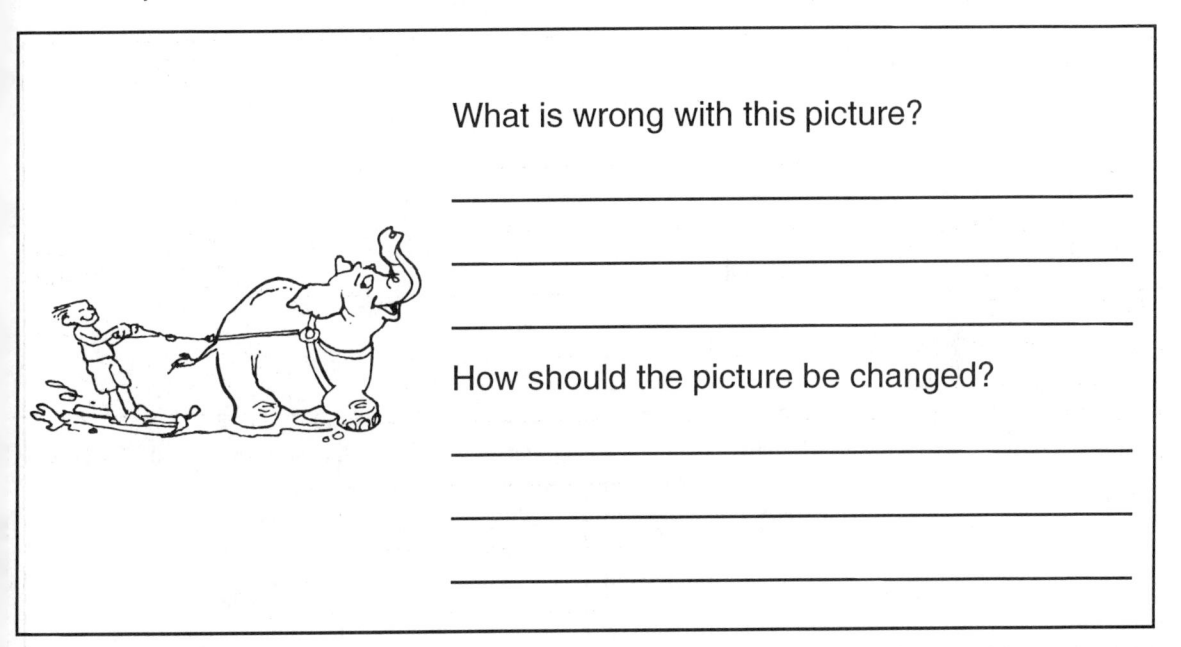

What is wrong with this picture?
_____
_____
_____

How should the picture be changed?
_____
_____
_____

What is wrong with this picture?
_____
_____
_____

How should the picture be changed?
_____
_____
_____

Here's My Order

Use the chart symbols to rank-order the items on each list.

Symbols for Rank-Ordering

☼ = 1st place or choice

☺ = 2nd place or choice

😐 = 3rd place or choice

😕 = 4th place or choice

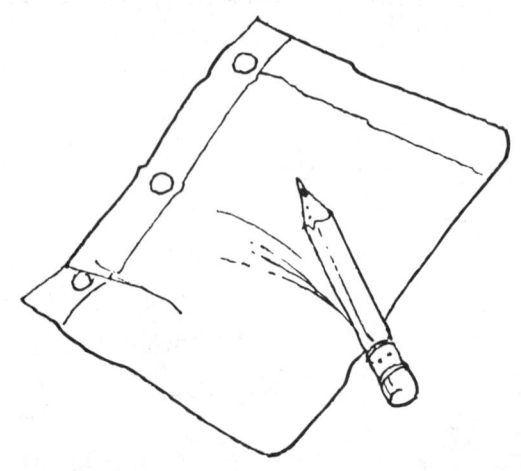

☹ = 5th place or choice

Time Spent in a Week on

_____ sleeping

_____ playing

_____ studying

_____ reading

_____ watching TV

Time Spent Each Week on Homework

_____ math

_____ spelling

_____ social studies

_____ science

_____ writing

Ways to Prepare for a Test

_____ alone in a quiet place

_____ with a friend

_____ with a parent

_____ with music on

_____ with people around

How You Like to Spend Recess

_____ alone in a quiet place

_____ inside for extra help

_____ reading inside or outside

_____ talking outside

_____ playing outside

Getting to Know You!

As you read about Sandy, Tanesha, and Kaitlin, you will get to know them. Use the information in the story to help you answer each question.

"Are you really going to try out for the lead?" Sandy inquired at lunch.
"Why not?" Tanesha replied between mouthfuls. "Nobody else in our class stands a chance. Besides, I take singing lessons. No one else does!" She tossed her long hair. She caught a glimpse of herself in the window and repeated the movement.
"Well, I...I was going to try out, too...." Kaitlin said, her voice trailing to a whisper.
"Good for you, Kaitlin!" Sandy smiled broadly. "I think I'll give it a try myself!"
"I just have trouble learning lines. And I'm scared of looking foolish," Kaitlin added.
"Oh, don't be afraid. There's nothing to it," said Tanesha as she sauntered off.

1. Which girl might be easily embarrassed? _____

    Support your answer _____

2. Which girl might spend the most time primping in front of the mirror every morning? _____

    Support your answer _____

3. Which girl might be more likely to help Kaitlin learn her lines? _____

    Support your answer _____

I Predict

When you say what you think will be the most likely thing to happen, you are making a **prediction**. Read each story. Below each story are two predictions about what might happen next. Choose the prediction that is *more likely* to happen. Then explain why on the lines that follow.

1. Sarah and Tim were baking brownies. They mixed all of the ingredients together, poured the batter into the pan, and put the pan in the oven. Then they cleaned up the kitchen. While they were waiting for the brownies to bake, they began to play a board game. Suddenly, Sarah smelled something burning.

    ○ Sarah and Tim ran into the kitchen, turned off the oven, and took the brownies out of the oven.
    ○ Sarah and Tim continued to play the game.

    _____
    _____
    _____

2. One day Jeremy was flying his new kite. Suddenly, a gust of wind blew the kite into the tree. Jeremy sat on the ground and began to sob. "Why are you crying?" asked a man. "My kite is up in that tree and I can't get it," Jeremy replied. "Will you help me?" The man sadly looked at Jeremy. Then he looked at the kite way up in the tree.

    ○ The man walked away.
    ○ The man got a ladder.

    _____
    _____
    _____